Caps and Crowns

By Amy Knapp and Illustrated by Brandon Jeffords

Requests for permission to reproduce any part of this book should be directed to:
Sandpiper Press • Post Office Box 35145 • Sarasota, Florida 34278
941.966.0290 voice/fax or 1.800.557.5333

Copies are available in better bookstores or may be ordered from **Sandpiper Press** by sending $19.95 plus $5.00 for shipping and handling.

ISBN 0-9658498-0-5

Library of Congress Catalog Card Number: 97-092225

Art Direction, Design, and Production by Joline Rivera

Printed by Worzalla Printing Company

For children everywhere . . . especially Sable and Montana.
Wear caps or crowns. I love you always.

Caps and Crowns celebrates children and what they do best —
observe, explore, experiment and play. I wish it could be bottled.
I want to thank my friends and family who have inspired me to
pursue worthy goals and high thinking. Joline — thank you for your
generous and talented spirit. Bodoni lives. AK

To my family... especially my younger brother Jeremy. BJ

Two sisters, Dexter and Aliena, lived in a
lovely little house in Kentucky where they
played together for hours and hours.

Their parents liked to watch how they held
hands and hugged often.

Dexter was seven. . .

and she loved ball caps . . .

and basketball . . .

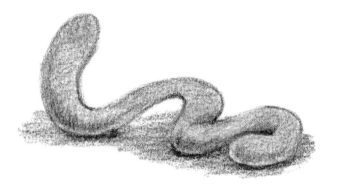

and didn't mind having dirt under her nails.

Aliena was five . . .

and she loved to wear crowns . . .

and dance ballet . . .

and hated having dirt under her nails.

Dexter's favorite color was black.

Aliena's favorite color was pink.

Sometimes Dexter would watch Aliena
dance, when Aliena didn't think
anyone was watching.

Sometimes Aliena would watch Dexter
shoot hoops, when Dexter didn't think
anyone was watching.

Aliena cheered for her sister at ballgames.

Dexter fidgeted through Aliena's dance
recitals but she loved to clap at the end.

One day Aliena asked Dexter if she wanted
to try her crown.

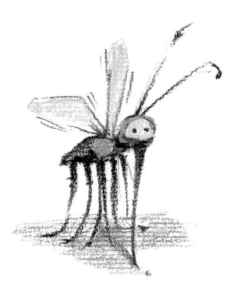

"No way!" shouted Dexter, as she scratched
her mosquito bites.

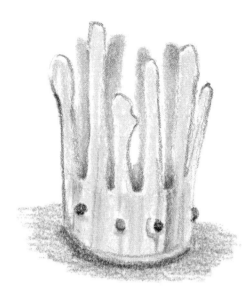

And then the sisters giggled. "Ya wanna
wear my cap?"

"Not me," said Aliena, brushing her long
silky hair. "I like crowns."

One day the sisters had a big fight.
There was a lot of yelling and they had to
go to their rooms.

Pouting, Dexter drew mean pictures with
black crayon.

Crying, Aliena shoved her face in her pillow.

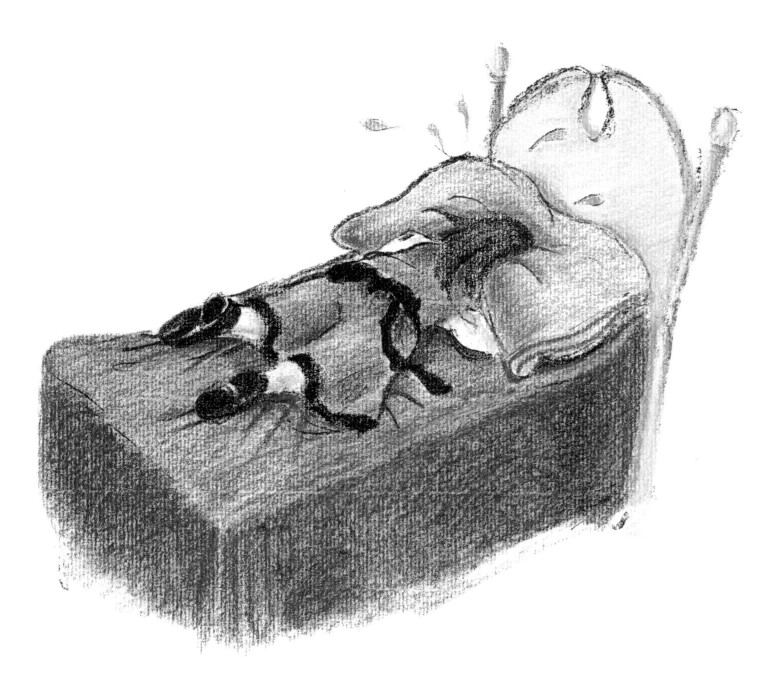

Eventually, Dexter was playing
basketball and Aliena was dancing again.

One rainy, miserable day while the girls
played separately, Aliena peeked through
the door to Dexter's room and said,
"Now, do you want to try my crown?"

"Your crown? Ummm . . . okay," said Dexter.
So Dexter took off her cap and Aliena gently
placed the crown on her head.

"This feels funny," Dexter said
laughing. "Here, try my cap." Dexter put
the cap on Aliena's head.

Aliena giggled, "I don't feel like me."

They pointed and laughed at each other . . .

then quickly changed headpieces.

"That was fun," they agreed.

The girls didn't know it, but their parents were watching and smiling. "Caps and crowns. That's our girls—caps and crowns.

Amy Knapp is a writer and mother. She lives with her daughters and their pets in Sarasota, Florida. Writing has been a hobby of Ms. Knapp's for many years but only recently has she dedicated her time to writing for children. Soon to be released books include *The Gate*, *Chi Chi*, and *The Color of Noodles*.

Brandon Jeffords is an illustration major at Ringling School of Art and Design in Sarasota, Florida. He has a background in musical theater and hopes to go into film animation.